Author:
Fiona Macdonald studied history at
Cambridge University, England, and at the
University of East Anglia. She has taught in
schools, adult education and universities, and
is the author of numerous books for children
on historical topics.

Artist:
David Antram was born in Brighton, England,
in 1958. He studied at Eastbourne College of Art
and then worked in advertising for fifteen years
before becoming a full-time artist. He has
illustrated many children's non-fiction books.

Series creator:
David Salariya was born in Dundee, Scotland.
He has illustrated a wide range of books and has
created and designed many new series for
publishers in the UK and overseas. David
established The Salariya Book Company in 1989.
He lives in Brighton, England, with his wife,
illustrator Shirley Willis, and their son Jonathan.

Editor: **Tanya Kant**

Editorial Assistant: **Mark Williams**

Published in Great Britain in 2010 by
Book House, an imprint of
The Salariya Book Company Ltd
25 Marlborough Place, Brighton BN1 1UB
www.salariya.com
www.book-house.co.uk

HB ISBN-13: 978-1-906714-23-9
PB ISBN-13: 978-1-906714-24-6

$ALARIYA

© The Salariya Book Company Ltd MMX

1 3 5 7 9 8 6 4 2

A CIP catalogue record for this book is available
from the British Library.

Printed and bound in China.

Visit our website at **www.book-house.com**
or go to **www.salariya.com** for **free** electronic versions of:
You Wouldn't Want to be an Egyptian Mummy!
You Wouldn't Want to be a Roman Gladiator!
Avoid Joining Shackleton's Polar Expedition!
Avoid Sailing on a 19th-Century Whaling Ship!

Avoid being
Joan of Arc!

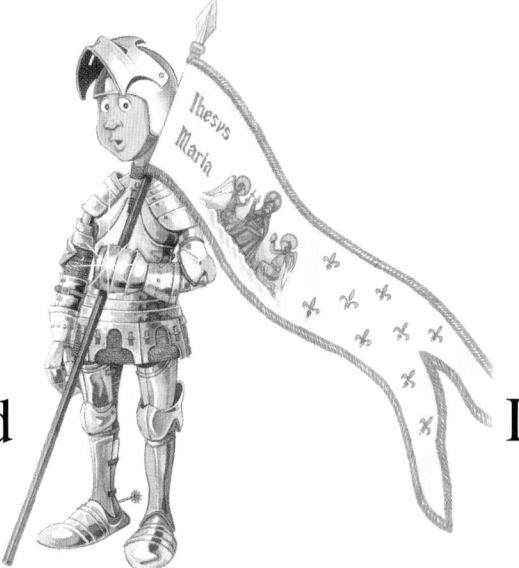

Written by
Fiona Macdonald

Illustrated by
David Antram

Created and designed by
David Salariya

The Danger Zone

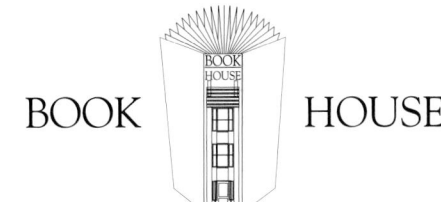

BOOK HOUSE

Contents

Introduction

The year? Around 1428. The place? A village in north-east France. And you? You're Joan, the daughter of peasant farmers. Not rich, not poor, just ordinary.

Like all the other local youngsters, you've grown up with fear and danger. Three rival armies are fighting in France. One of your cousins has been killed in a battle, and the village church – next door to your family's house – has been burnt down by enemies.

So far, you've managed to stay safe. But now your life looks risky. Why? Because you have a hope, a dream, a secret, sacred mission: to rescue France from its enemies!

You're young (just 16) and unknown. You can't read or write, and have not been trained to use weapons. You don't understand politics or know how to plan a battle. But you're utterly convinced that you can save your country. How will you do this?

I have a mission! But how can a girl like me save an entire country?

Dutiful daughter

Your parents are respectable and hard-working: your father keeps sheep and grows corn, your mother cooks, sews, cleans and looks after the household. You're from a large family! You have a sister and three brothers, all older than you. For as long as you can remember, everyone has expected that you'll grow up to be like them: busy, helpful and stay-at-home.

Your parents – and the Christian Church – say that, as a girl, you must be modest, gentle and obedient. They expect you to marry one day, and become a dutiful wife and mother.

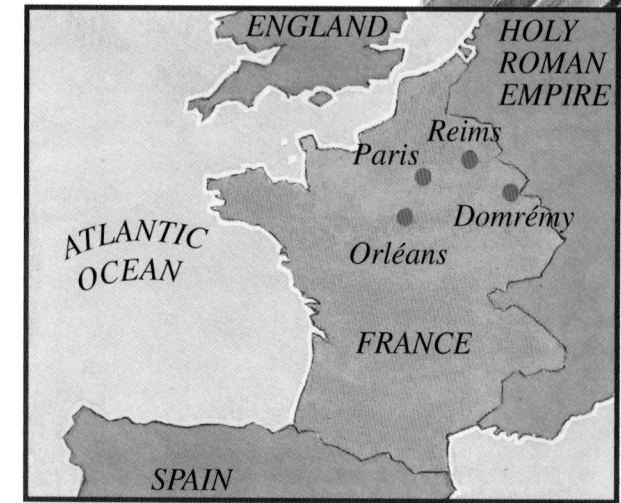

DOWN ON THE FARM. Your home is in the village of Domrémy, in the region of Lorraine. It's good farming country, with vineyards on the hillsides and rich green pastures beside the wide river Meuse.

A good girl

ALONG WITH most people in Europe at this time, you've been brought up as a Christian. Local priests and your mother have taught you to say prayers.

YOU HAVE LEARNED sewing and spinning so that you can make clothes and household linens. You're proud of these skills.

TO SHOW YOUR FAITH, you make garlands of flowers to decorate holy statues.

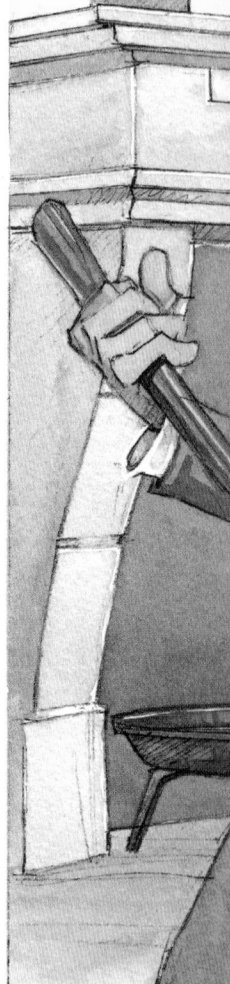

I want to be a good daughter, but there must be more to life than housework!

Handy hint

Be helpful around the house! As a peasant girl, you don't have much power. You depend on your family for food, clothes and shelter.

In the war-zone

You cannot remember a time without war. In fact, there has been fighting between England and France for almost a century – it will be known as the Hundred Years' War. Most of the battles have been fought on French soil. Hundreds of peaceful villages have been attacked, and countless families have seen their farms ruined. Vast areas of the countryside are now poor. Your home village is right between lands ruled by sworn enemies – the King of France and the Duke of Burgundy (who is friendly with the English). Earlier this year, you and your family had to run for your lives when Burgundian soldiers attacked. You hid for two weeks in the nearest town, until it was safe to return.

WAR HERO? The English still boast about their brave King Henry V. In 1415, he won a famous victory against the King of France at the Battle of Agincourt. But, six years ago, he died of dysentery, aged 35. Now his little son is king of England – and claims to be king of France, too.

God help us!

GREEDY LOOTERS. Invading troops will steal everything they can carry. If you have animals, they'll cook and eat them!

ANGRY ATTACKERS. Rough soldiers will threaten women and children. Stay out of their way if you can!

CRUEL DESTROYERS. Before marching on, enemies will set fire to houses, farms and barns, leaving villagers homeless.

9

Rival rulers

You and your family are loyal supporters of the King of France. But 40 years of quarrels among the French royal family, plus bad decision-making by French King Charles VI, mean that your country is now in danger. England's kings are claiming the right to rule France because they are descended from a French princess. The English now control half the country.

King Charles VI died in 1422, just six years ago. Now his son, young King Charles VII, has vowed to drive the English out.

The story so far:

1. CONFUSED KING. King Charles VI has a nickname – Charles the Mad. For many years, the poor king did not know who he was. Sometimes, he thought he was made of glass!

I'm his brother!

I'm feeling rather fragile today...

Domrémy
Paris

English lands

Charles's land

4. LEFT IN CHARGE. By 1417, Charles VI was too ill to rule France. His son, Prince Charles, took over the government, aged only 14. At first, he was helped by the Duke of Burgundy.

5. THE ROYAL ROWS continued for years. In 1419, Charles's royal friends plotted against the Duke of Burgundy and murdered him. This made the Burgundians hate French royals – and like the English more.

6. NOW, IN 1428, France is a divided country. Charles VII, England and Burgundy all control different areas.

2. THE ROYAL FAMILY could not agree who should rule while Charles VI was ill. Charles's brother, Louis of Orléans, quarrelled with Charles's cousin, the Duke of Burgundy.

The king is not fit to rule! I should be in control!

Well, I'm his favourite cousin!

Handy hint

Don't trust your neighbours! The outskirts of your village, just across the river, have been conquered by the Burgundians.

3. IN 1407, the Duke of Burgundy ordered the murder of Prince Louis of Orléans. This made French royals hate the Burgundians.

Burgundian ands

7. FRENCH ROYAL TROOPS are depressed and disorganised. How can they hope to win against English knights on horseback, or arrows fired from longbows, England's deadliest weapon?

8. CHARLES VII has been king of France since 1422, when he was only 19 years old. He's managed to stay in power for the past six years – but his advisors are still arguing among themselves.

Hearing voices

s a child, you did not understand the reasons for the war that was wrecking your homeland. You just got on with life, helping your mother around the house and looking after the farm animals. Then, one day, about 4 years ago, something extraordinary happened…

You were by yourself, in your father's garden, when suddenly, there were voices! They held you spellbound with their sweetness and power. You looked everywhere, but there was no-one to be seen – just dazzling light from the sun. Then the voices stopped, and the sun's rays dimmed. Confused, frightened and awestruck, you ran home, crying.

Handy hint

Don't tell anyone! The Church and the villagers are suspicious of people who claim to see visions or hear voices. They might say you're mad – or a witch.

Who do the voices belong to?

AT FIRST, you don't know who spoke to you. But in the next four years, you hear the voices again – many, many times. At last, you think you recognise them:

ST CATHERINE of Alexandria (below). A wise and holy young woman, killed for being a Christian. She helps people in danger.

ST MARGARET of Antioch. A martyr, killed for her faith, she protects women. Legends tell how she escaped, unharmed, from the belly of a dragon!

SAINT MICHAEL. Prince of angels and a mighty warrior, he protects the French army.

13

An urgent mission

You're a sincere Christian. You've always tried to follow Church teachings – and obey your parents, too. But now, in 1428, you're about to horrify – and frighten – everyone who loves you. Why, Joan, why? You say that your voices are telling you to take action. You must obey them – it's a holy command!

You, Joan, a peasant girl aged 16, must leave home, lead an army, defeat the English, and take young King Charles VII to the ancient royal city of Reims, which has been under English control since Charles became king. There, Charles can be blessed by the Church and officially crowned King of France, like all his royal ancestors. That, you say, will prove that God wants him to be king.

YOUR VOICES are very precious to you – and, at first, rather worrying. So you keep their precise words all to yourself, and never repeat them to anyone.

Can I really lead an army?

14

Who does she think she is?

Handy hint

Stick to your nickname! It's *La Pucelle* ('the Maiden'), and it might protect you. It means that you are holier than other women, a bit like a nun.

SOME PEOPLE don't think that you or your voices are holy. They believe in a sinister pagan prophecy which says that a 'maiden from the oakwoods' (the French countryside) will one day save France. Are you that maiden? If so, you're deeply dangerous!

Why you?

HOURS OF PRAYER have convinced you that the voices you hear come from Heaven. You feel sure that God approves of your plan. But will anyone else believe you? And why have you been given this difficult and dangerous task?

Joan is a wonder! She's the maiden from the oakwoods!

Royal meeting

Your mind is made up. You must go to the royal court! But girls cannot travel alone, so you ask a male relative to ride with you. French soldiers are suspicious and send you back home, but you keep on trying. At last, two French nobles take you to the king. They think you might be useful.

In 1429, you kneel before young Charles VII, and beg him to let you help France. King Charles looks worried and alarmed. Who are you? Can he trust you? He sends you to be questioned by Church lawyers. They think you are honest and trustworthy – so Charles lets you join his army!

Poor Charles needs all the help he can get. They say he has only 4 gold coins left.

BANNER BRIGHT.
You want to fight with
a banner (a sign of
leadership), not with
a sword. Charles gives
you a holy banner,
decorated with a picture
of Jesus Christ and two
angels. You're also
given a suit of armour
to protect you.

Ihesvs
Maria

Handy hint

Travel in disguise. Dress for
your journey as a servant
boy. That way, the
rough, rude
soldiers will be
less likely to
pick on you!

BEST BEHAVIOUR. You 'purify'
the French army by sending soldiers'
girlfriends home and making the men
say their prayers.

Saving a city

To have a hope of ruling France, young King Charles must keep the city of Orléans under his rule. It's the last French city still unconquered, and controls the rich Loire valley, called the 'garden of France'.

Can Orléans survive an English siege?

SOLDIERS DEFENDING the walls of Orléans are in great danger, but they must keep watch in case of an attack.

Woosh!

Ihesus Maria

Ow!

Thunk!

I don't know which way to look!

English soldiers have surrounded Orléans, trapping its citizens inside the city walls. The city's food and water supplies are running low, and disease is spreading. English troops have also captured the twin towers guarding Orléans' main gateway. You've been wounded, but your troops need you. You must stop the English from breaking into the city and killing its inhabitants!

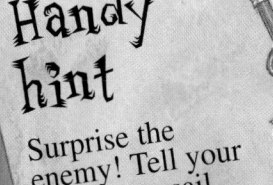

Handy hint

Surprise the enemy! Tell your soldiers to sail down the river and attack the English unexpectedly from behind.

WAR CAMP. English troops set up camp beside the city, so that they are always close by, ready to attack.

SHARP-SHOOTERS. English archers fire arrows at defenders who dare to look over the battlements.

WRECKED. English armies have burnt the local countryside, so there is little food for Orléans' inhabitants.

COMMAND AND CONTROL. For safety, English officers give orders from a nearby monastery.

FIREPOWER. Huge stone balls, fired from English cannons, can smash city gates.

LOOK OUT! English patrols stop Orléans' citizens from sending for help or trying to escape.

POISON WATER. English soldiers have polluted nearby wells, so Orléans' defenders can't get fresh water.

The King is crowned

With you to lead and inspire them, the French army have saved Orléans. King Charles VII is extremely grateful, but his enemies are furious, his courtiers are astonished, and Church leaders are suspicious. How can French soldiers be commanded by a girl with no army training? How on earth did you lead them to victory?

Don't let cruel words worry you. Your next task is to lead Charles's army through lands controlled by the English to the city of Reims. There, Charles VII can be crowned at last, like all his ancestors. Coronation is an ancient, holy ceremony; the Church teaches that it turns a king into a ruler, blessed, approved and guided by God. Until the coronation, many people will say that Charles is not a real king.

En route to Reims

TWANG! The English have gangs of archers hidden along your route, waiting to fire at you.

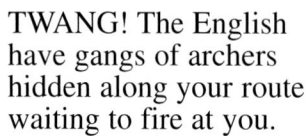

CLINK! England has paid Burgundy to recruit more men to fight against you.

CRASH! You are hit by a stone thrown by an English soldier. You must stagger to your feet and continue.

Donk!

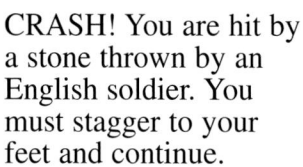

CHARGE! An English army blocks your path. But your soldiers attack, scatter them, and reach Reims. You've made it!

Isabeau, queen of France, has had a tragic life. Her husband Charles VI was mentally ill and most of her 12 children died. In desperation, she made friends with the Burgundians, and agreed with them that England should rule France. To back their claim, she may even have spread rumours that her son, Charles VII, was not her husband's child.

Handy hint

Charles VII's coronation is probably the happiest day of your life. Accept the praise showered on you by the French. You will also want to give thanks to God.

Mission accomplished!

Sensing doom

It's winter, 1429. Your leg has been badly injured by a crossbow bolt. Your men have won a few small battles, but have not been able to recapture Paris, the French capital, from English armies. King Charles VII's advisors are trying – but failing – to make peace with Burgundy. They want to make sure that Charles keeps control of the lands you won along the way to Reims.

The winter weather is too cold for any army to fight, so you rest for a while. Your leg gets better, but you fear that you will soon be betrayed and captured. Your voices are warning that this will happen before St John's Day (24 June) 1430.

1. SURROUNDED! On 23 May 1430, as you supervise your army, Burgundian soldiers creep up and surround you.

Grab the girl!

It's all your fault!

4. SQUABBLE, SQUABBLE. Charles VII's courtiers quarrel among themselves, accusing each other of betraying you. In fact, their bad advice on how to fight the war has led you into danger.

5. RANSOM! Charles VII offers a ransom (a rich reward) for setting you free. The Burgundians refuse, and sell you to the English for 10,000 gold coins.

2. COME THIS WAY. The soldiers drag you off your horse and take you to their leader, Lionel of Wandomme.

You're coming with us!

Handy hint
Wear boys' clothes in gaol! The soldiers will be less likely to attack you. Trousers are also warmer in a damp, draughty cell.

3. HOORAY! The Burgundians rejoice at your capture, while your French soldiers are devastated.

Woo-hoo!

It's pay-back time.

6. DESPERATE! You try to escape by jumping from a tower around 20 metres (70 ft) high. You land in a muddy moat and are injured, but survive.

7. IN CHAINS. You are locked in an army prison, surrounded by rough soldiers. As a girl, you ought to have women gaolers, but the English want you to suffer.

A terrifying trial

The judge and lawyers all support England. They are too frightened – or greedy – to treat you fairly.

The English want revenge! You have stopped them from completing their conquest of France, and made sure that Charles VII has been crowned king instead of his English rival. Angry English soldiers take you to Rouen in north-west France, a city they control. There are clear rules, respected by English and French, for dealing with captured enemies. Usually, important prisoners like you are ransomed, then set free. But the English want you to be punished as severely as possible. They accuse you of breaking the Church's holy laws – a very serious crime. Your trial, in a Church court, begins in February 1431. It's a cruel farce.

Forced confession

The court finds you guilty – of course! After the trial, you are forced to sign a 'confession' which you cannot read and do not really understand. It says that you have broken Church laws, that you have asked the Church to forgive you and that you promise never to do wrong again.

What am I signing?

The English accuse you of witchcraft – a deadly sin. They declare that your voices are devils, not saints.

The Church claims that your male clothes are evil, unnatural and against God's laws. If you disobey God, you're damned!

Handy hint

Beware! The lawyers will try to trap you into saying something sinful. Think carefully before you answer!

There are no witnesses to speak up for you, and no French lawyers to defend you.

You ask the court to write to the Pope (the head of the Church) to give you a fair trial. Your request is denied.

Life – or death?

The English are still angry. They've not yet managed to kill you! The Church gives criminals a chance to reform. So, obey Church laws and you'll survive – though you'll spend the rest of your life in prison. Of course, you'll have to stop meddling in politics – and put on women's clothes.

To you, all this is intolerable. You cannot do what the Church commands. You must obey your voices, and speak out to help France. At first, you wear women's clothes, to please Church lawyers. But male prisoners attack you, so you dress like a man again. Now you've broken Church laws for a second time. Your fate is sealed. You must die!

Glorious memory

You die on 30 May 1431, holding a little cross handed to you by a kindly peasant. You are just 19 years old. You have suffered a grave injustice and a terrible death. But your short life has changed the course of history. For a while, the English will try to make everyone forget about you. But in 1449, they will be driven out of Rouen. The long war will be over at last, and France will be at peace.

Soon after, the Church will look back with horror at your trial, and declare that you should never have been killed. It will call you a holy martyr – and a saint.

Still honoured!

YOU HAVE SHOWN what ordinary people – and women – can achieve. Tourists visit your home at Domrémy, to show respect.

Handy hint

Follow Joan's example! Always be true to what you believe in.

IN 1920, you were made a saint by Pope Benedict XV. People say you work miracles, to guide, help and heal.

YOUR STORY has inspired great paintings, statues, films, plays and poems.

IN FRANCE, you are a national hero and a proud symbol of independence. Christians everywhere admire your faith and courage.

IN JOAN'S TIME, people believed in voices from Heaven. Today, some people share that belief, while others are doubtful. Whatever we think, Joan's story warns us that war brings great injustice – and terrible suffering.

Glossary

battlements The wall at the top of a castle that has narrow spaces built into it for shooting at enemies.

bolt (crossbow) A sharp, deadly metal spike, like a short arrow. Bolts are fired from a crossbow – a powerful, trigger-activated bow.

Burgundy During Joan of Arc's lifetime, an area of Europe that included parts of modern-day France and Switzerland.

coronation A religious ceremony in which a monarch's heir has a crown placed on their head, is blessed by the Church, and is declared to be the lawful king or queen.

courtier A noble man or woman, or high-ranking official, who lives in a king's or queen's household, provides companionship, gives advice and performs useful duties.

dysentery An illness carried by infected water; it causes severe sickness and diarrhoea.

farce A ridiculous or pointless event, such as a trial for a person whom the court is already determined to find guilty.

heir A person who inherits (is given) money, a title or property after the owner's death.

Hundred Years' War A series of wars, fought between England, France and Burgundy, for the right to rule France. They lasted for 116 years, from 1337 to 1453.

longbow The most important weapon used by English foot-soldiers during Joan of Arc's time. It was about 2 metres (6 ft) tall and made of tough, springy wood. It could fire an arrow up to 100 metres (330 ft).

martyr A person prepared to suffer or die for their religious beliefs.

miracles Religious, supernatural events.

monastery A community where monks or nuns live and devote their time to God. In Joan of Arc's time, monasteries were centres of art and learning; some also included hospitals.

pagan A word used by people in Joan of Arc's time, and later, to describe pre-Christian religious beliefs and practices.

peasant A poor farmer or farm worker.

Pope The head of the Roman Catholic Church.

prophecy A statement that claims to predict the future.

ransom A large sum of money paid to enemies to set a war prisoner free. In Joan of Arc's time, rich prisoners were usually set free after their families paid a ransom. Poor prisoners, whose families could not afford to pay, were often killed.

saint A dead man or woman honoured by Christians for their holy life and their devotion to religion. Some Christians believe that saints perform miracles to help the living.

siege A way of making war: an attacking army surrounds an enemy town or city and keeps the occupants trapped inside until they surrender or starve to death. The besieging army may also try to fight its way into the city, to kill the occupants and seize their property.

spinning Twisting animal hair (wool) or plant fibres (flax) to make a strong, smooth thread for weaving or sewing.

visions Religious or spiritual supernatural experiences.

Index